One fine day, FLIP was in a FUNK

A story about friendship, empathy, and sadness

Written by
Tamara Sheppard

Illustrated by
Maham Ali

The Flipping
Feelings Series

Foreword

Dear Parents, Educators and Caregivers:

Welcome to an extraordinary children's book that will ignite young hearts and minds with the superpowers of kindness, empathy, and compassion. By embracing and accepting the feelings of others, we'll learn to offer empathy and support, creating a world where understanding and connection thrive. Get ready for a captivating tale that celebrates the beauty of emotions and empowers children to make a positive difference.

Let's get started!

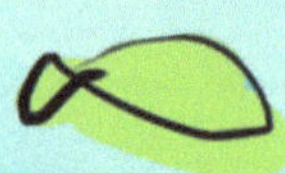
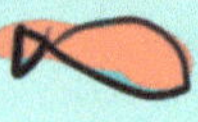

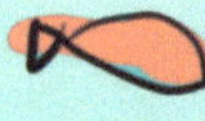
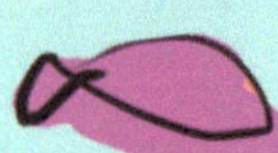
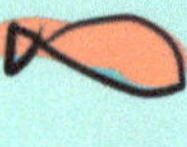

First published in 2023 by Dash Academy Press
Written by Tamara D. Sheppard
Illustrated by Maham Ali
Book design by Bryony van der Merwe

ISBN: 978-1-7779917-1-5

For every little person
who is in a
FUNK,
sometimes.

One fine day,
Flip was in a
FUNK.

When Flip looked at the sunny skies,
all Flip could see was

GREY.

When Flip looked for a seashell,
all Flip could find was
BEIGE.

When Flip was asked to
dance and play,
Flip answered,
"NOT TODAY,"

AND...

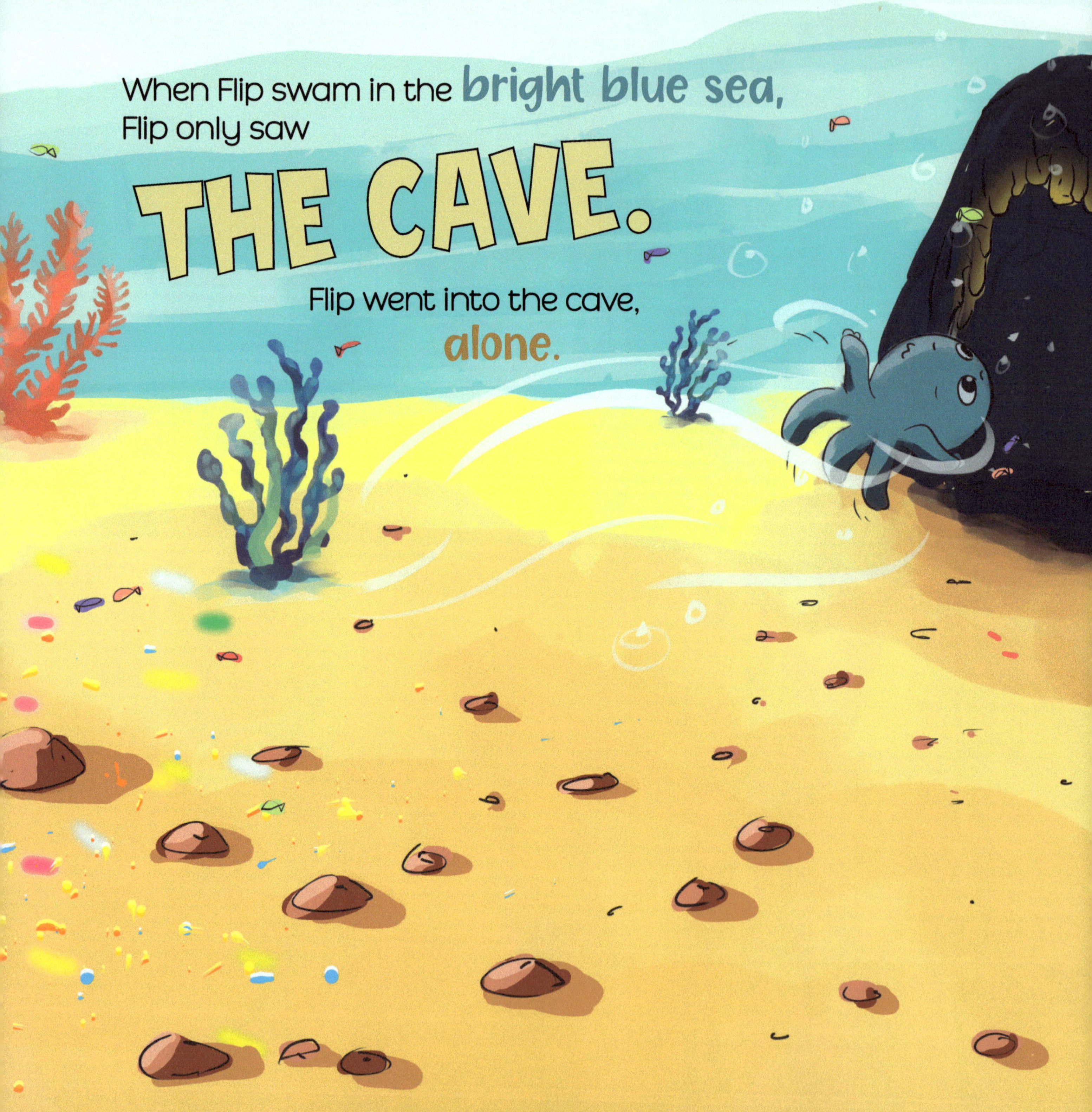

When Flip swam in the bright blue sea,
Flip only saw
THE CAVE.
Flip went into the cave,
alone.

The cave was deep.
The cave was dark.
Flip could not see the sky.
The cave was still.
The cave was quiet.
Flip settled in and sighed.
Ho Humm

Flip's friends swam by and saw
the cave that Flip had settled in.

They **called to Flip,**
"Come out, come out;
your cave looks **SAD** and **GRIM."**

First, **Clownfish** peeked into **the cave**,
then quickly **backed away**,

"Your cave is **dull** and **boring**;
let's go out;

enjoy the day!"

"NO,"
said Flip politely.

"I'll give you sweets," sang Jellyfish,
"your favourite snacks and treats."
"I'll leave them here;
outside your cave,
come out, then you
can feast!"

"NO,"
said Flip, gratefully.

"Oh, Flip," whined Whale, "this cave of yours is getting on my nerves."
"I feel sad that you're in there. Come out; I'm getting worried."

"NO,"
said Flip, tenderly.

"SNAP OUT OF IT," barked Angelfish,
"come out of your cave NOW."
"Just grin, stand tall, lift up your chin,
and push your troubles down."

"NO,"
said Flip, quietly.

"Then we give up," Flip's friends all cried,
"we don't know what to say."

"No **tricks** or **treats**, no **bribes** or **pleads**,
will make **Flip feel okay.**"

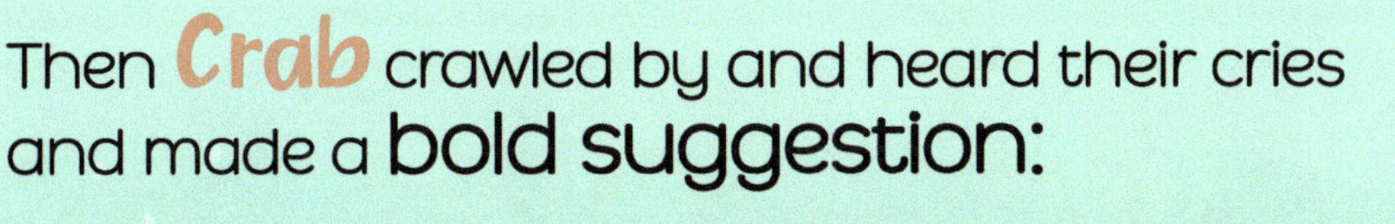

Then **Crab** crawled by and heard their cries
and made a **bold suggestion:**

"**Flip's in a funk** and needs **our love.**
Let's try EMPATHY
and COMPASSION."

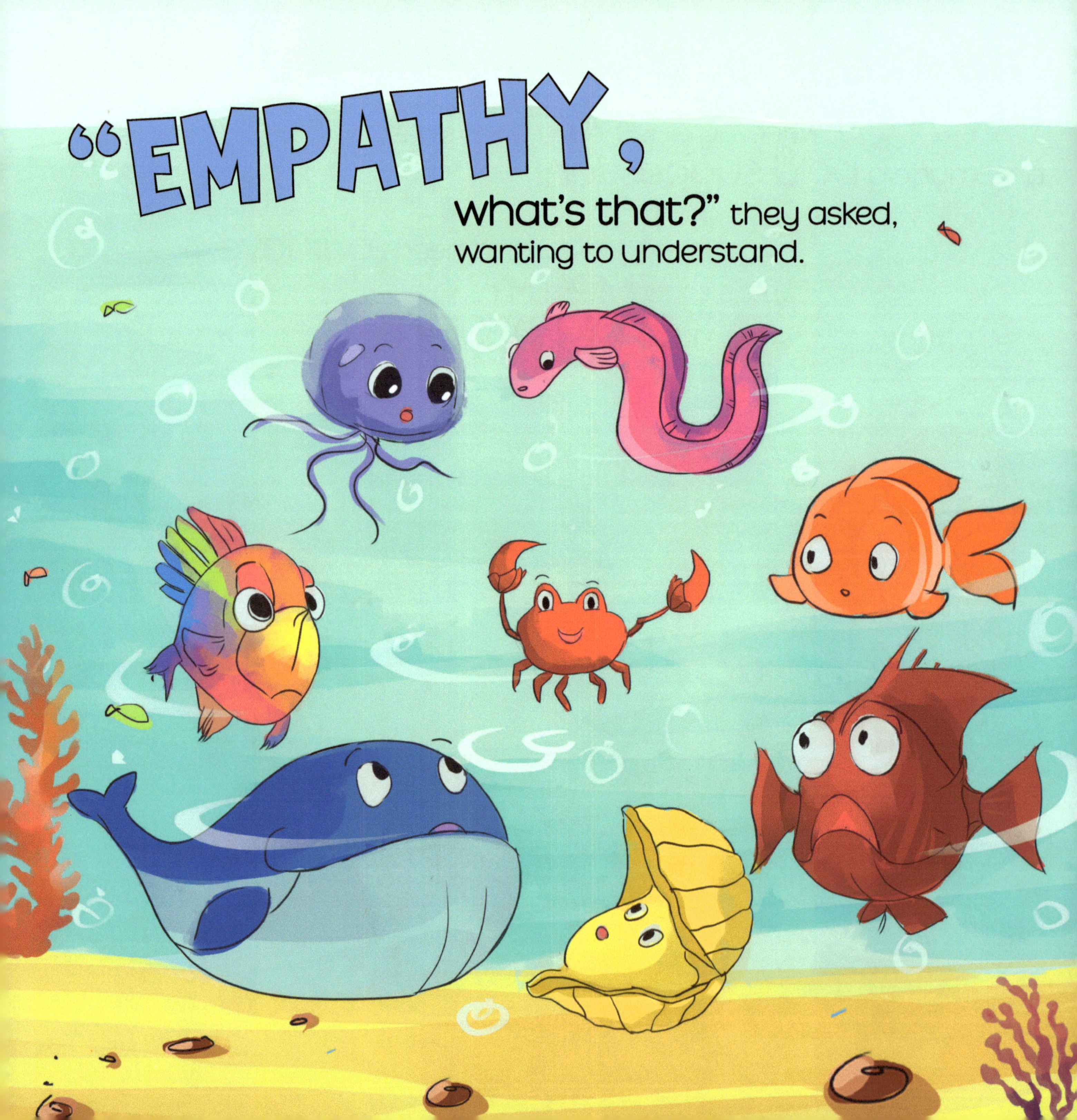

"EMPATHY,
what's that?" they asked,
wanting to understand.

So, Crab explained that
EMPATHY is
kindness, love,
and action.

"I will try EMPATHY,"
said Eel.

First, Eel wriggled to the cave,
then did something
remarkable,

Eel did not stay outside but swam
INTO the darkness.

said Eel to Flip, "may I sit with you a while? I understand you're in a **funk** and find it hard to smile."

"YES,"
whispered Flip.

And as they sat together in the darkness,
the cave became a little brighter.

"I will try EMPATHY,"
chirped Parrot fish.

Next, Parrotfish slid into the cave;
and offered Flip

A HUG.

"It's cool inside your cave,
dear Flip; some tea may
warm you up."

"YES,"
agreed Flip.
And as they sat side-by-side in the shadows,
sipping their tea, the cave seemed
a little warmer.

"I will try EMPATHY," declared Clam.

When Clam climbed into Flip's damp cave, Clam heard Flip's **lonely cries**.

soothed Clam, "I'm here for you. Everyone cries sometimes."

"YES,"
sniffed Flip.

After some time, Flip began to talk,
and Clam quietly listened.
Then Flip felt a little bit lighter.

"WELL DONE,"

cheered Crab, "your **EMPATHY** is showing
Flip **you care.** It lets Flip know you
understand the feelings we all **SHARE.**

Then Crab crawled into Flip's **sad cave**
and softly said, "Hello." "May I come in
and play with you? It's hard to be **alone.**"

"Your friends all know
what it feels like to be in a

SAD FUNK.

We know that it is tough for you.
It feels like you're stuck."

"But funks don't last forever;
the blues will float away,
and when you feel ready, you'll
swim out of your cave."

"OKAY,"
nodded Flip.
And when Flip felt understood, loved, and cared for, Flip's funk did start to drift away.

Flip's friends have learned the **lesson** of what to **do** and **say,**
when they see a friend is in a funk and swims into a cave.

They won't **peek** in
from safe outside.

They will not **tease**
with treats.

They will not **whine**
or worry.

They will not **yell**
or screech.

With **empathy** and **compassion,** they will seek to understand
the feelings that Flip feels and lend a **helping hand.**

They will **spend time**
in the darkness.

They will sit **close**
side-by-side.

They will offer
loving kindness.

and a **chat**
from time to time.

Receiving kindness, love, and action
from an **empathetic friend**
may help Flip see the **sunny sky**
and choose to dance again.

The
END.

I am sincerely grateful you read this book with a child you care for. Empathy is an essential Emotional Intelligence skill. Learning to respond to someone in pain with empathy builds loving relationships and healthy human connections.

Here are four simple ways to model empathy.

1. Listen without judgment or response.
2. Acknowledge their emotions. A person in pain wants to be seen, heard and believed.
3. Show interest. Honour their search for connection with you.
4. Be supportive. Offer meaningful actions, like a hug, a cup of tea or a tissue.

This book is part of THE FLIPPING FEELINGS SERIES. For additional books, toys, and tools to support learning Emotional Intelligence with Flip, visit me at DashAcademy.ca "Training that Matters"

About the Author
Tamara D. Sheppard, MSc.

Tamara lives in Alberta, Canada, with her husband, Dean. They have three grown sons, one sweet daughter-in-law, and an adopted dog named Toby. Tamara's family loves to travel the world and meet interesting people. For fun, they like to scuba dive and have met Flip and all of Flip's friends in the ocean.

DashAcademy.ca